UP-GRADE!

Light relief between grades

Spaß und Entspannung mit leichten Originalstücken für Klarinette *Erster Schwierigkeitsgrad*
Plaisir et détente avec des pièces originales simples pour clarinette *Niveau 1*

Pam Wedgwood

FABER *ff* MUSIC

Foreword

Up-Grade! is a collection of new pieces and duets in a wide variety of styles for clarinettists of any age. This book is designed to be especially useful to students who have passed Grade 1 and would like a break before plunging into the syllabus for Grade 2.

Whether you're looking for stimulating material to help bridge the gap between grades, or simply need a bit of light relief, I hope you'll enjoy **Up-Grade!**

Pam Wedgwood

© 1998 by Faber Music Ltd
First published in 1998 by Faber Music Ltd
3 Queen Square London WC1N 3AU
Cover design by Stik
Music processed by Jackie Leigh
Printed in England by Caligraving Ltd
All rights reserved

ISBN 0-571-51819-2

To buy Faber Music publications or to find out about the full range of titles available
please contact your local music retailer or Faber Music sales enquiries:

Faber Music Limited, Burnt Mill, Elizabeth Way, Harlow CM20 2HX
Tel: +44 (0)1279 82 89 82   Fax: +44 (0)1279 82 89 83
sales@fabermusic.com   fabermusic.com

Contents

4

1. Take It Easy

Gently ♩ = 88

Pamela Wedgwood

2. Land of Hope and Glory

Maestoso (majestically) ♩ = 88

Edward Elgar

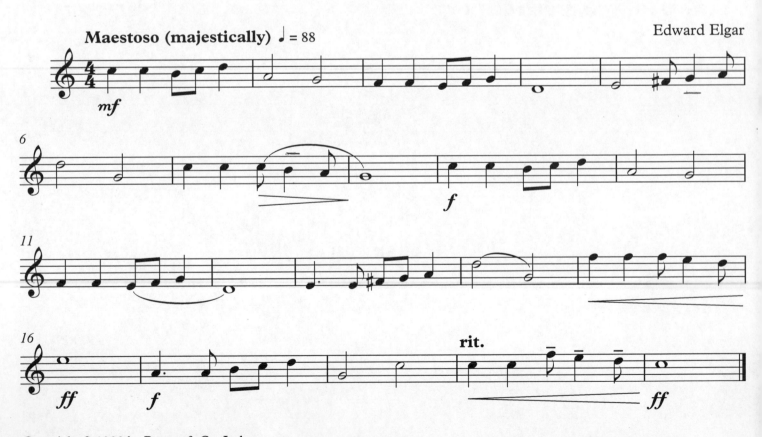

3. Apple Pie Waltz

Pamela Wedgwood

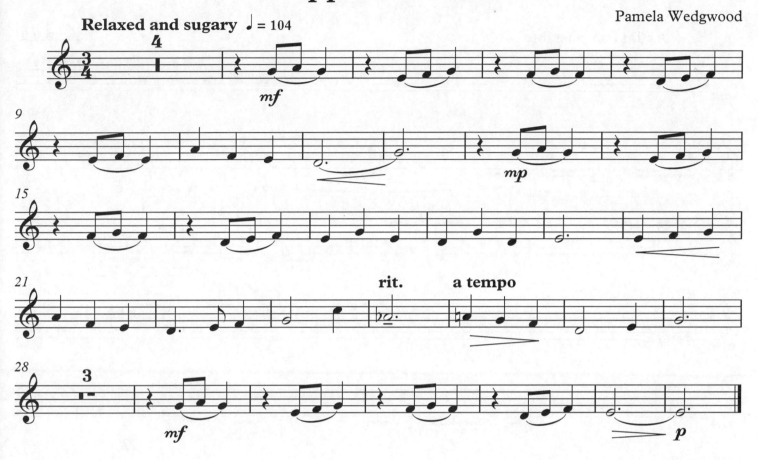

4. Banana Boat Song

Traditional

5. What shall we do with the Drunken Sailor?

As fast as possible

Traditional

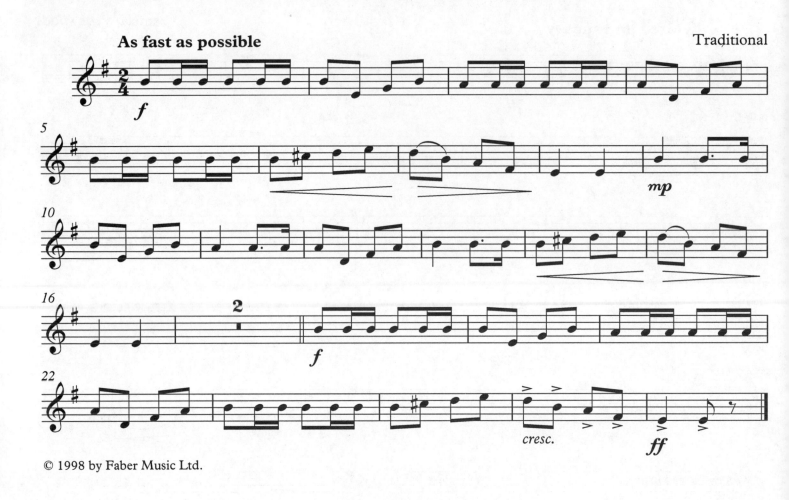

6. La Donna e Mobile

Allegretto ♩ = 120

Giuseppe Verdi

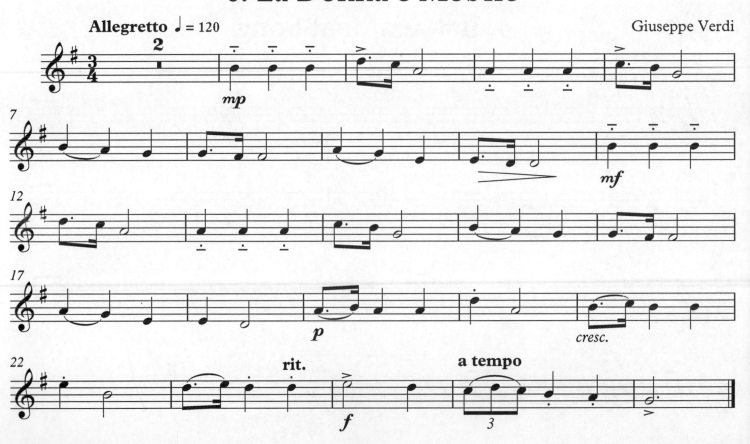

7. Rosemary and Thyme

Pamela Wedgwood

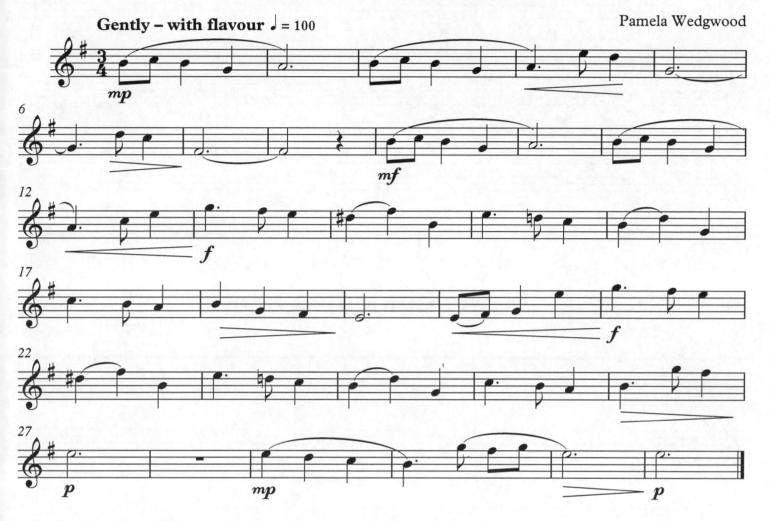

8. Greensleeves

attrib. Henry VIII

8

9. Can Can

Jacques Offenbach

10. The Contented Frog

Pamela Wedgwood

* Use side trill key for B

11. Theme from 'The Teddy Bears' Picnic'

J.W. Bratton

12. Off to the Sun

Pamela Wedgwood

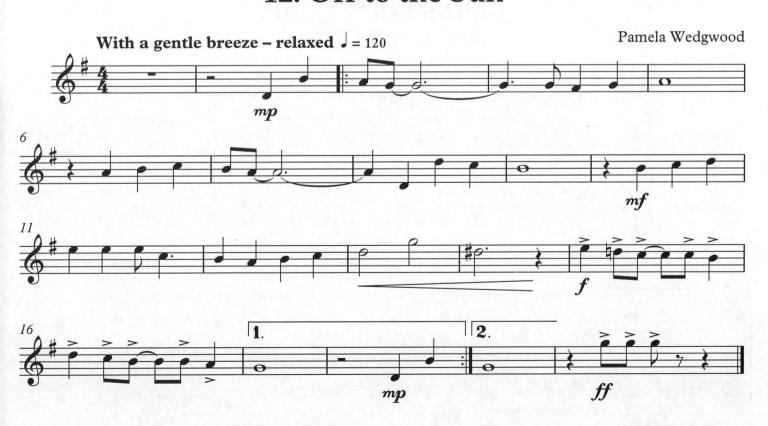

13. Chinese Take It Away

Moderately – sweet and sour ♩ = 120

Pamela Wedgwood

14. It's Duet Time!

two duets in D minor

Pamela Wedgwood

Don't rush – count carefully! ♩ = 112

Pamela Wedgwood

15. Fandango (a duet)

Pamela Wedgwood

UP-GRADE!

Light relief between grades

Spaß und Entspannung mit leichten Originalstücken für Klarinette *Erster Schwierigkeitsgrad*
Plaisir et détente avec des pièces originales simples pour clarinette *Niveau 1*

Piano accompaniments

Pam Wedgwood

FABER *ff* MUSIC

Foreword

Up-Grade! is a collection of new pieces and duets in a wide variety of styles for clarinettists of any age. This book is designed to be especially useful to students who have passed Grade 1 and would like a break before plunging into the syllabus for Grade 2.

Whether you're looking for stimulating material to help bridge the gap between grades, or simply need a bit of light relief, I hope you'll enjoy **Up-Grade!**

Pam Wedgwood

© 1998 by Faber Music Ltd
First published in 1998 by Faber Music Ltd
3 Queen Square London WC1N 3AU
Cover design by Stik
Music processed by Jackie Leigh
Printed in England by Caligraving Ltd
All rights reserved

ISBN 0-571-51819-2

To buy Faber Music publications or to find out about the full range of titles available
please contact your local music retailer or Faber Music sales enquiries:

Faber Music Limited, Burnt Mill, Elizabeth Way, Harlow CM20 2HX
Tel: +44 (0)1279 82 89 82   Fax: +44 (0)1279 82 89 83
sales@fabermusic.com   fabermusic.com

1. Take It Easy

Pamela Wedgwood

2. Land of Hope and Glory

Edward Elgar

4

3. Apple Pie Waltz

Pamela Wedgwood

4. Banana Boat Song

Traditional

5. What shall we do with the Drunken Sailor?

Traditional

6. La Donna e Mobile

Giuseppe Verdi

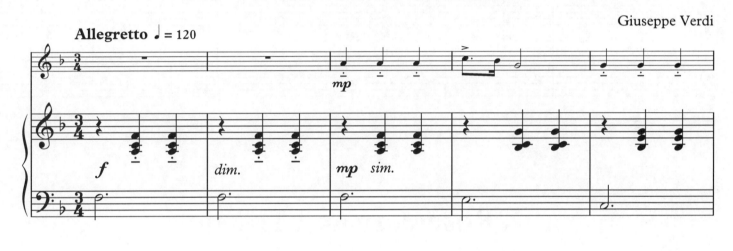

7. Rosemary and Thyme

Pamela Wedgwood

8. Greensleeves

attrib. Henry VIII

9. Can Can

Jacques Offenbach

10. The Contented Frog

Pamela Wedgwood

11. Theme from 'The Teddy Bears' Picnic'

J.W. Bratton

12. Off to the Sun

Pamela Wedgwood

13. Chinese Take It Away

Pamela Wedgwood